RAINBOW REVOLUTIONS

POWER, PRIDE, AND PROTEST IN THE FIGHT FOR QUEER RIGHTS

JAMIE LAWSON   EVE LLOYD KNIGHT

Crocodile Books, USA
An imprint of Interlink Publishing Group, Inc.
www.interlinkbooks.com

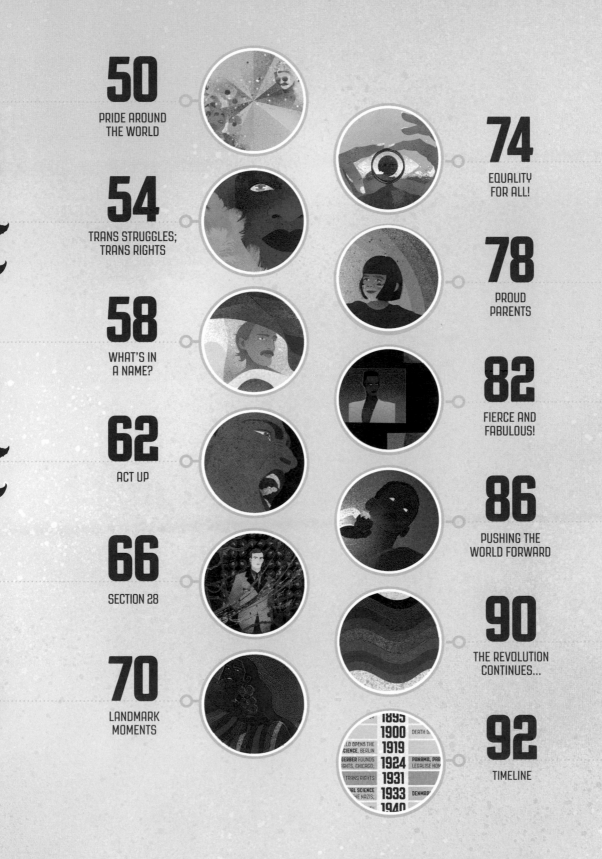

THIS BOOK IS ABOUT THE FIGHT FOR QUEER RIGHTS.

"Queer" is a complicated word. It's used today to describe anyone who doesn't easily fit into the place carved out for them in the mainstream, heterosexual world. Originally it was a slur, an insult, that was used to draw attention to someone's difference and make them feel ashamed, or threatened. That still happens sometimes, but queer has now become one of a number of words that people of many diverse orientations and genders can use to describe themselves and their community. Alongside queer you may find the words lesbian, gay, bisexual, and trans, which are often represented together as LGBTQ+.

The queer community hasn't always existed. For a long, long time queer people were, and in many parts of the world continue to be, cruelly oppressed. Laws making it legal for gay men and women to exist openly are very recent developments in many countries, and in many others being queer is still illegal. In some places it's punishable by death. Even in places where LGBTQ+ people are protected by law, they can run into discrimination and prejudice on a daily basis. Being queer in those circumstances is very lonely, and very scary.

Homophobia can take a number of different forms, from being denied service in a bar or restaurant to being refused treatment in hospital; from being made to feel uncomfortable holding hands with a partner to verbal or physical assault. Trans people in particular have often been the targets of horrendous and tragic acts of violence. LGBTQ+ parades and marches can themselves become targets of aggression, disrupted by homophobic violence from those who refuse to accept the sight of queer people celebrating their identities.

And yet, people still organize parades, and people still come. The rainbow flag—the best recognized symbol of the LGBTQ+ community—still flies, even in places where being seen holding it can lead to arrest, torture, or worse. Some years ago, queer people around the world realized that speaking out in the face of homophobic abuse was better than keeping quiet, however scary that might be.

This book is about the way queer people learned that lesson. It's about the struggles they faced, and continue to face, across history. It's about the birth of the queer rights movement, and the community that emerged as a result. It's about the brave individuals and groups who stood up and told the world how unfairly they were being treated, and about how they blazed a trail for others to follow. This book is about the ways queer people found to connect to each other, and build a world for themselves within a larger social system where they were not welcome. It's about legendary activists who took a stand, and about how they gave others courage to take their own stands, however big or small.

Because no matter its size, every act of resistance against the mainstream is in itself a revolution.

The Stonewall Riots

On June 28, 1969,
around one o'clock in
the morning, New York
City Police raided the
Stonewall Inn, a bar
in Greenwich Village,
New York, USA.

Stonewall was a gay bar; a place where lesbians, gay men, bisexual, trans, and other queer people went to dance, have fun, and express themselves.

That wasn't easy to do in New York at the time. Laws about same-sex relationships and how people were supposed to look and behave made being queer extremely dangerous. Sex between two men or two women was illegal in New York, and people could be stopped by the police and arrested if they were wearing fewer than three items of clothing that the police thought were appropriate for their gender. Even the smallest act, such as men holding hands in public, could result in a prison sentence. Against this background, it was very hard for queer people, and trans people in particular, to feel free to look how they wanted to look, or to be the person they wanted to be.

Many bars and businesses refused to serve queer people and could fire their employees if they even suspected they might be queer. People had to keep their sexuality secret and pretend to be straight, because if anyone found out they could lose their jobs, their friends and even their family.

> **Many bars and businesses refused to serve queer people and could fire employees if they suspected they might be queer**

Gay bars like the Stonewall Inn were safe spaces where everyone could look as much like a man, woman, or anything in between as they liked, where people could step out of a world in which being themselves was impossible and spend some time among friendly faces and bright lights.

They were lively, welcoming places, where, for a few hours, queer people could escape the hatred, bullying, and abuse they experienced in their day-to-day lives.

But wider society didn't like the idea of having queer people in the City, and didn't want them to have places to gather. The NYC Police regularly raided the gay bars in Greenwich Village, looking for reasons to close them down—and on June 28, they tried to close the Stonewall Inn. A police van pulled up outside, and officers poured into the bar, pushing and shoving people around. Customers who resisted, or who the police simply didn't like, were arrested and bundled outside to the van in handcuffs.

> **She looked at the silent faces of the crowd around her and started shouting at them, asking them to help, asking them why they were standing still**

The freedom of the evening was over; the straight world had come to shut down the party, to show queer people again that they weren't welcome.

People started to get scared. And then they got angry.

Two leading figures of the queer community realized it was time to make a stand. Marsha P. Johnson, a drag queen and black trans woman, and Sylvia Rivera, a Latina trans woman, were both well-known and well-loved for being loud and proud on the New York queer scene. Sylvia had been born in New York City, while Marsha had lived in New York since 1963, and both were well used to mistreatment at the hands of the police. When they saw what was happening to their friends at Stonewall, they decided they'd had enough. They began shouting at the police, screaming at them to stop, encouraging the crowds to act, to stand up against the harassment and bullying.

While police continued to push customers out of the bar, and to arrest those who resisted, a crowd began to gather. Onlookers watched in silence as drag queens and other people they knew and loved were carted into the van. At one point, the police pulled Stormé DeLarverie, a black queer woman, out of the bar. DeLarverie was furious and struggled with the police. She looked at the silent faces of the crowd around her and started shouting at them, asking them to help, asking them why they were standing still: "Why don't you do something?". People began to shout back at the police, yelling for them to let her go. The anger spread through the crowds. People started to move, to organize.

As Marsha, Sylvia, and others began to fight back, people joined them. Over the next six days, thousands of queer people took to the streets to protest against the hatred and mistreatment they'd experienced all their lives.

This uprising became known as the Stonewall Riots, and its impact was to be far greater than anyone could ever have imagined.

> **Over the next six days, thousands of queer people took to the streets to protest against the hatred and mistreatment they'd experienced all their lives**

A Queer New World

To understand the source of the outrage and anger that led to Stonewall, we need to dig a little further back in history ...

During the Victorian era, European culture developed strict ideas about sexuality and about what was proper and desirable for men and women to do.

Society was suspicious of "otherness," and regarded queer people as deviant or abnormal. Queerness was often associated with disease, and was approached as a problem to be dealt with, or cured. Europeans then carried those prejudices with them as they claimed other parts of the world for their own. As they imposed colonial rule around the world, they took their laws, their norms, and their prejudices with them.

Because of those prejudices, for over a hundred years before the Stonewall Riots, queer people in many parts of the world had lived in fear of being exposed. In lots of countries, being queer was illegal, and for a long time anyone who was suspected of being anything other than heterosexual had been persecuted, imprisoned, or even killed.

But the Riots were not the first demonstration of resistance from the queer community. One of the earliest campaigns for gay rights occurred in the nineteenth century, in Germany.

Born in 1825, Karl Ulrichs was a German writer who became the first openly queer person to speak publicly in support of gay men. Unusually for the time, Ulrichs had been very honest about his attraction to other men for many years. He worked hard to

Karl Ulrichs was a German writer who became the first openly queer person to speak publicly in support of gay men

change the attitudes of society toward people like him, and has become known as one of the earliest queer activists.

Today, words like trans, bi, or gay are well-known, but in the 1800s there weren't any words that queer people could use to describe themselves. While they were called many things, none of those terms were positive and most were usually associated with immorality and disease. Ulrichs tried to change that by inventing a new vocabulary to describe queer people. Ulrichs called a man who, like him, was attracted to other men an Urning (or Uranian). A woman attracted to women he called an Urningin, and he had words for bisexual and intersex people too. While Ulrichs' words have gone out of fashion and are seldom used today, they represent the first time a queer person tried to name themselves in a positive way—a very powerful thing to do.

In 1867, at the Congress of German Jurists in Munich, Germany, Ulrichs made a remarkable speech. Arguing that society's treatment of queer people was unjust and unfair, Ulrichs said that laws used to send gay men to prison should be changed. While Ulrichs wasn't able to overturn these laws, the fact that he was prepared to stand up in front of politicians and judges to make his case made many people in the audience start to take the issue seriously. In the decades following his speech, a greater tolerance began spreading through Germany. People started openly discussing sex and sexuality, and police in Berlin enforced anti-gay laws less often.

By 1919, Magnus Hirschfeld, a German doctor concerned about the wellbeing of his gay patients, had opened the Institute of Sexual Science in Berlin, Germany, which became a safe place for queer people to meet, talk, and find support or refuge if their families had turned against them. Soon, magazines, films, and books about queer lifestyles appeared, and in the 1920s, a vibrant, thriving queer world started to open up in Berlin, particularly within the cabaret scene.

Cabaret was a type of playful live performance, full of bright lights and laughter. Different acts would perform, from dancers and singers to clever comedians, all dressed in bold, glamorous costumes. Cabaret played with conventional gender rules: women would wear clothes that were normally reserved for men, like tailcoats and top hats, while men might perform in glitzy, flamboyant dresses, feathers, and make-up. It allowed queer people to throw off society's strict rules, and granted them free expression in an atmosphere of fun and creativity.

> In the 1920s, a vibrant, thriving queer world started to open up in Berlin, particularly within the cabaret scene

The Pink

Triangle

But the bright lights of queer
Berlin suddenly went out in
the 1930s, with the rise
of the German dictator
Adolf Hitler and the
Nazi Party.

The Nazis had risen to power in the aftermath of World War I, when Germany, along with much of Europe, was rebuilding itself.

They were a far-right, fascist group whose ideology was built on the idea of German superiority, and a narrow view of history that emphasized conquest and military power.

When the Nazis came to power in Germany, their aim was to remove these groups from society

The Nazis hated anyone they regarded as different. They hated people who were Jewish, people who weren't white, people who they considered foreign, people with disabilities, and people who were queer. When the Nazis came to power in Germany, their aim was to remove these groups from society. They were locked up in concentration camps, where they were beaten, tortured, and killed.

Although being queer in Germany had been illegal for a long time, the work begun by Ulrichs, and continued by Hirschfeld and others, had helped to make German society more tolerant and open. The Nazis, however, put an end to that tolerance and began to strictly enforce the anti-gay laws. They compiled lists of individuals who were suspected of being queer, and arrested them. They sought out information from doctors, friends, family, and anyone else who queer people thought they could trust. Everyone was scared of the Nazis, so they turned on each other.

Suddenly queer people couldn't trust anyone.

In the concentration camps, gay men were marked with a pink triangle. Viewed as the lowest of the low, they were treated horrifically. Queer women were branded with a different symbol, a black triangle, to identify them as "social deviants." The exact number of queer people who died in the camps is not known, but somewhere between 5,000 and 15,000 men were sent there for being gay.

The Nazis were eventually defeated in 1945, at the end of World War II, and the concentration camps were liberated. Those who had survived were finally released. Everyone, that is, except for the men marked with pink triangles.

They were often sent straight back to prison to see out the rest of their sentence, because even though the war was over, the tolerance of the 1920s was long gone and queer people were once again stigmatized and oppressed. Many countries in Europe still had laws against what they knew as "homosexuality." So even those who managed to avoid arrest had to deal with a world full of prejudice and homophobia.

One of those men was Pierre Seel.

In 1941, at only 18 years old, Seel had been arrested and convicted for homosexuality. He was sent to a concentration camp, where he suffered abuse and humiliation.

After the war was over, he returned home to his native France, but his family and friends knew why he had been arrested and imprisoned by the Nazis, and shunned and excluded him because of it. While homosexuality had been legal in France since the 1790s, life was still very hard for those who were open about their sexuality, so, like other queer survivors, Seel didn't tell his story for fear of further punishment. He carried his memories of the camp with him for decades, never feeling able to talk about them, until he finally stood up to tell of his ordeal in the early 1980s. People were shocked and horrified by what he and men like him had been through, and they began looking for ways to commemorate these forgotten victims of the Nazis.

Seel published his story in 1994, and became a well-known activist, campaigning for recognition and remembrance for the queer victims of the Holocaust until his death in 2005.

> While homosexuality had been legal in France since the 1790s, life was still very hard for those who were open about their sexuality

The Sip-in Protest

After World War II, attitudes started to change radically. The atrocities committed under the Nazi regime had sent shockwaves around the world, and the death and destruction of the war itself forced people to look at society in a new way.

It was obvious to everyone that the world couldn't survive another global conflict, and the sheer horror of the war pushed many countries to swear they would never let it happen again.

While politicians negotiated treaties with each other to ensure peace, new social movements started to emerge as people came together to try to build a better world.

Despite this, life for queer people, along with many other minority groups, remained very difficult. In lots of countries, traditional rules about how men and women should behave and dress persisted, and were strictly enforced. Those who didn't conform were treated as if they were mentally ill or criminal. Many queer people continued to live secret, hidden lives to avoid losing their jobs, being abandoned by their loved-ones, or ending up in prison.

But a few brave activists found ways to fight back. In the United States, stirrings of this resistance

But a few brave activists found ways to fight back

had already begun in 1920s Chicago with the German immigrant Henry Gerber's Society for Human Rights, the first activist group in the USA for gay men.

Gerber had emigrated to North America in 1913, at the age of 21. At 25, he was committed to a psychiatric hospital for "homosexuality," so saw first-hand how American society treated queer men like him. Enlisting in the US army during World War I, Gerber was stationed in Germany, where he remained for a few years after the war was over. There, he found the playful, liberating queer scene in Berlin and returned to America full of ideas for creating something similar. Sadly, he couldn't find a way to reach out to the queer people he knew were living secret lives in America, and the

Society for Human Rights collapsed after less than a year.

After World War II however, things began to change. A lot of queer soldiers who had served in the military during the war were discharged once the conflict was over, and found themselves living in cities in and around military bases. Often unable or unwilling to return home, many of those ex-soldiers decided to stay put and start a new life for themselves. Cities like New York, Chicago, and San Francisco developed large queer communities. Queer people found each other, and social and activist groups started to form.

One such group, known as the Daughters of Bilitis, was the first civil rights organization for queer women, and was founded in San Francisco in 1955 by lesbian couple Del Martin and Phyllis Lyon. Lasting until the 1970s, the Daughters of Bilitis hosted hugely popular public meetings, and its newsletter, *The Ladder*, became an important community focus for queer women across North America.

But it wasn't until 1966, three years before the Stonewall Riots, that a group called The Mattachine Society, established by political activist Harry Hay to campaign for gay men's rights, made a protest so public that it caught people's attention.

Many of the bars in New York at that time refused to serve anyone who was queer. So on April 21, 1966, the Mattachines went into a popular bar, announced that they were gay, and calmly asked for a drink. Instead of going alone, they brought news reporters with them. When the bar refused to serve them, a storm of media attention erupted, and the public was forced to confront the ways queer people were being treated. Some were shocked with the bar's actions, others thought they were justified. But regardless of whether people agreed or disagreed with the bar's decision, finally people were talking openly about it. Queer rights had become front page news.

This small act of protest, which became known as "the sip-in," led to an important legal victory, and bars in New York were no longer allowed to turn away customers based on their sexuality. The Mattachines showed that queer people could engage in a form of resistance simply by making themselves visible.

> When the bar refused to serve them, a storm of media attention erupted, and the public was forced to confront the ways queer people were being treated

Stepping Into The Light

The Mattachines, like Gerber's Society for Human Rights, took a very particular approach to queer liberation that seems quite conservative by today's standards ...

Their aim was to demonstrate that anti-gay laws were unfair because queer people could be trusted to behave responsibly.

The Mattachines wanted to show that they were no different from anyone else, and that they could have a quiet drink in a bar just like straight customers would. Queer people were regarded as deviants, as mentally ill or dirty, and these early activist groups, for the most part, wanted to dispel those prejudices. Like many other queer activist groups at the time, they wanted to be part of mainstream culture, and set out to show that they were no different from anyone else—that they could fit in if they were allowed to. This approach of wanting to fit in is known as "assimilationist."

But the Stonewall Riots changed all that. Stonewall brought home how badly society was willing to treat queer people, and showed the queer community around the world that they could force change by being

Around the world, queer people were starting to mobilize and raise their voices loudly against their oppression

loud, by being proud, and by pushing back. Rather than trying to argue that they were the same as the mainstream, straight community around them, many queer activist groups started to emphasize that they *were* different, and that this was nobody's business but their own. Queer communities started to demand recognition. They wanted to have *their* culture, *their* history, *their* differences recognized. Rather than changing themselves to fit in to a narrow and discriminatory culture that wouldn't give them room, they wanted the culture to change to allow them free expression within it.

After Stonewall, queer liberation and radical activism really started to gain momentum. In the USA, the Gay Liberation Front picked up the cause and continued to protest loudly against intolerance and prejudice. The GLF quickly spread overseas, appearing in the UK and Canada in 1970. A chapter of the Daughters of Bilitis became Australia's first gay rights group, swiftly followed by the Campaign Against Moral Persecution. Around the world, queer people were starting to mobilize and raise their voices loudly against their oppression.

On the first anniversary of the Stonewall Riots, to mark that important moment in history, queer communities paraded the streets of New York and Chicago to commemorate them. The idea of celebrating the bravery of the people at Stonewall began to spread to other cities around the world, including Paris, France, and London, UK; and "Gay Liberation Day" became an annual event, marked by an organized march, and loud protests against oppression and prejudice.

At this time, a number of important queer people stood up to lead the fight for equality, among them Harvey Milk. Originally from New York, Milk had moved to San Francisco in 1972 and opened a camera shop in the Castro, the heart of the city's gay village. He was charming and popular, and his shop became a social hub, where queer people would come to meet, and

He stood up and proudly told the world he was gay, encouraging others to do the same. He called this "coming out"

talk about politics and resistance. Milk soon became a popular community leader in San Francisco, and began talking publicly about queer rights and freedoms. Unusually, Milk directed a lot of his ideas towards the LGBTQ+ community itself, because he believed its people held the keys to their own liberation. He knew that if queer people stepped out of the shadows and made themselves visible, then the straight world would have no choice but to accept them. He wanted queer people to be open about who they were, so that they could unite and demand acknowledgement and equality. He stood up and proudly told the world he was gay, encouraging others to do the same. He called this "coming out."

In 1977, Milk became one of the first openly gay men to be elected to a political post in the USA. It was an amazing victory and a moment of triumph for the queer community.

But it was to be short-lived. Only a year later, on November 27, 1978, Harvey Milk was shot and killed in his office in City Hall, San Francisco. However, despite this tragedy, Milk's message of visibility and pride had taken root in the queer world and his death was marked by a candlelit vigil, attended by thousands of supporters.

"Your Silence Will Not Protect You"

Audre Lorde

Harvey Milk was not alone in seeing "coming out" as being key to queer liberation. Throughout the 60s and 70s, and up until her death in 1992, Audre Lorde was using her voice to urge queer people, particularly women, to speak up and make themselves heard.

Lorde was a writer and civil rights activist who dedicated her life to fighting inequality and injustice wherever she saw it.

A gifted poet, Lorde spun words together into beautiful, powerful poetry in order to comment on the world around her, and to make people think about the oppression and prejudice they faced and their own roles in oppressing others.

> She described herself as "black, lesbian, mother, warrior, poet," and strove to have all the different aspects of her identity recognized

Born in 1934, Lorde lived through many decades of world-changing activism. She was a vocal participant in the civil rights and feminist movements, joined the protests against the Vietnam War in the 1960s, and became a well-known figure in New York's queer scene. She published several books of poems, all reflecting different periods of her life and describing her experience as being a black, queer woman in the United States. She publicly came out as a lesbian in her second volume of poems, *Cables to Rage*, in 1970.

Lorde understood that people's identities were complex and multifaceted, and challenged society's tendency to categorize people into separate groups. She described herself as "black, lesbian, mother, warrior, poet," and strove to have all the different aspects of her identity recognized.

Lorde looked around at a world in which women, black people, and queer people were treated as second class citizens or worse. She saw activist and social justice movements that supported these separate groups, but realized that because each one only represented a part of her identity, she'd never wholly belong to any of them. She wasn't just a woman, for example: she was a *black* woman, so she would have to deal with racism from women's groups and sexism from black activist groups. She wasn't just a black woman either, but a *queer* black woman, so was confronted with oppression and prejudice from inside the community of black women as a consequence of her sexuality.

Lorde saw that the only way that she, and people like her, could be truly represented would be if activist groups started to come together and build alliances between themselves. She wanted women's and queer groups, for example, to confront the racism that often circulated inside them, so that they could build close connections with black activist groups. She thought these alliances were key to universal liberation, because they would allow all oppressed people to come together and fight for their freedom in a world where most of the power was held by straight, white men.

At a feminist conference in 1979, Lorde explained that this idea of community and celebration of diversity was central to her vision for the future: "Without community there is no liberation ... But community must not mean a shedding of our differences, nor the pathetic pretense that these differences do not exist."

> "Without community there is no liberation ... But community must not mean a shedding of our differences, nor the pathetic pretense that these differences do not exist"

Lorde realized that mainstream society wouldn't change unless it had to. She saw first-hand that powerful people would ignore the difficulties faced by minority groups unless they were directly confronted with them. She urged others like her to step forward, to raise their voices and be clear about the way they were being treated by society; to point out bigotry and prejudice wherever they came across it. She believed strongly that oppressed groups needed to find their own voices, so that they could stand up to the people who were persecuting them, push back against the powerful, and shout them down if they needed to. She used every ounce of her skill as a writer to point out injustices, and kept up a rallying cry against them, urging people to find their own words, their own way of expressing how hard life was for them.

Above all, she understood that staying silent in the face of bigotry was not going to change anything. She wrote about how speaking out could only make things better, because silence would, at best, merely keep things as they were.

For Lorde, and those she still inspires, the act of speaking out, of saying loudly and clearly how and when you've been bullied or hurt, is not only a powerful act of resistance, but also necessary to protect and empower yourself.

Herstory

Despite the contribution and efforts of key female figures like Marsha P. Johnson, Sylvia Rivera, and Audre Lorde, queer liberation movements are often associated solely with men. Women are frequently left out of the story.

But trailblazing women are a vital part of queer activism and were challenging discrimination and prejudice long before gay rights groups were up and running.

In the worlds of literature, art, and academia, as well as in activism itself, strong, powerful women have confronted the sexism, homo-, and transphobia that runs through many modern societies.

In the early twentieth century, Gertrude Stein was breaking boundaries and pushing against social norms as an author, artist, and poet. American born, Stein lived in Paris with her partner Alice B. Toklas. Stein wrote a great deal about her relationship with Toklas, often disguising this so that her work would be published. Despite this, the women lived openly as a couple for many years, and hosted regular social gatherings, known as salons, where they would entertain well-known writers and artists such as Ernest Hemingway and Pablo Picasso. Stein's work is very important to the development of feminism,

and her partnership with Toklas is one of the most famous lesbian relationships in history.

> In her personal style as well as her paintings, Kahlo played with gender rules, presenting herself as both masculine and feminine at the same time

At the same time, the artist Frida Kahlo was working in Mexico. Painting in brilliant bold colors, she produced a series of beautiful self-portraits that depict and celebrate her identity as a mixed race, disabled, bisexual woman. In her personal style as well as her paintings, Kahlo played with gender rules, presenting herself as both masculine and feminine at the same time. Since her death she has become an internationally famous queer feminist icon, and her influence on the worlds of art and fashion can still be seen today.

Between the 1920s and 1970s, fellow artist Hannah Gluckstein defied gender norms in British and American society by refusing to be described in terms of he or she. Instead,

Gluckstein insisted on being known simply as Gluck. From an early age, Gluck chose to have short hair and refused to dress in the way society expected, preferring to wear "men's clothes." An innovative and strongly influential artist, Gluck's style and paintings challenged society's rigid beliefs about gender.

But it isn't only queer female artists and writers who have fought for their liberation; women in many other walks of life have spoken out against intolerance and hate.

American anthropologist Margaret Mead shocked the world with her first book *Coming of Age in Samoa* in the late 1920s. The book was the result of several years of fieldwork by Mead, and described the ways in which young women in Polynesian societies lived their lives. Mead told stories about empowered women, who could choose their own sexual partners whenever they wanted. This was so different from the way women in American and European society were expected to behave that people were appalled, but it forced them to reflect on their own culture and acknowledge that things could be different elsewhere. Mead's work laid the foundations for a great deal of research about gender and sexuality that followed, and she was an important figure in the new feminist movements of the 1960s. While Mead herself had three marriages, each with men, her longest and most intimate relationship was

> **Mead told stories about empowered women, who could choose their own sexual partners whenever they wanted**

with her friend and mentor, Ruth Benedict. Letters between the two, written while Mead was overseas in Samoa, reveal an intense, beautiful, and deeply romantic connection.

The year 2000 saw the death of queer activist Ruth Ellis. Ellis, an African American woman, was born in 1899 to parents who lived through the last years of slavery. Following emancipation, her father had become the first African American mail-carrier in her home state of Illinois. Her life spanned three centuries, and she was a first-hand witness to enormous social changes that took place during the twentieth century as the result of two world wars and coordinated social activism. She experienced the birth, struggles, and triumphs of the civil rights movement, the rise of feminism, and of course the battle for queer liberation. At age 20, Ellis met Ceciline "Babe" Franklin, who would become her partner for the next 30 years. Together, the two women offered support to the growing LGBTQ+ community in Detroit, Michigan, and offered their home as a safe haven to African American gays and lesbians in particular. Ellis was also a formidable activist, and following Stonewall she was often invited to give speeches at queer events and festivals. At the time of her death, Ellis was 101 years old. She is a legendary figure in the queer community, and is considered to be the oldest known "out" lesbian.

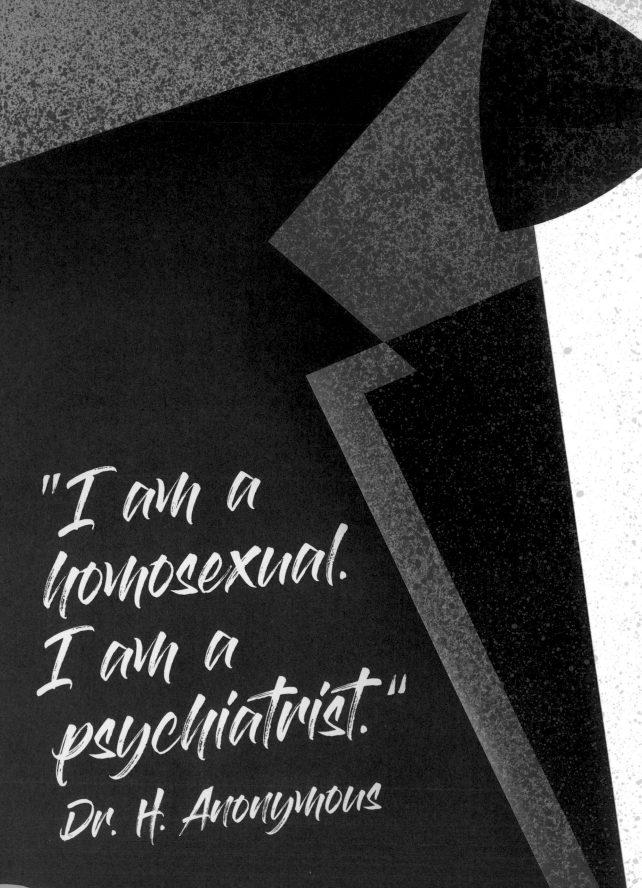

"I am a homosexual.
I am a
psychiatrist."
Dr. H. Anonymous

In 1972, a man took to the stage to address an audience of American psychiatrists. He was dressed unusually. Over a shirt and large bow tie, he wore a baggy, shapeless formal jacket with wide lapels. His hair was covered by a dark, curly wig, and his face was hidden behind a strange mask. When he spoke into the microphone, his voice was disguised electronically.

He had been introduced to the audience as Dr. H. Anonymous.

This is how he began:

"I am a homosexual. I am a psychiatrist."

Dr. Anonymous's real name was John E. Fryer. He had been a practicing psychiatrist in America for a decade before he put on his disguise and made his speech.

Announcing publicly to a room full of his fellow doctors that he was gay was a massive risk for Fryer, both professionally and personally. The term homosexual had, for over a hundred years, been associated with mental illness—used to describe something that was wrong with people—and doctors were expected to "cure" homosexuals through various forms of invasive therapy.

At the time Fryer stood up to make his announcement, homosexuality was officially listed in The American Psychiatric Association's (APA) book of mental illnesses. The word "homosexuality" had been used by the Victorians to describe something that they thought was an illness, and this idea was still prevalent in the 1970s. It meant that queer people couldn't be honest about who they were when they needed medical help in case their doctor started trying to treat them for homosexuality, instead of whatever was actually wrong. Psychiatrists themselves couldn't be openly queer, because they would have been considered too "sick" to work in the profession.

Fryer wanted to change that. He belonged to a small group of queer mental health professionals who kept themselves and their identities secret—the Association of Gay and Lesbian Psychiatrists. Together they had agreed that someone needed to speak publicly about the issues that queer psychiatrists and patients faced. Their ultimate aim was to have "homosexuality" removed from the APA's book of mental illnesses. Fryer had volunteered.

He told the audience what it was like for the queer men and women who worked in psychiatry, how difficult their lives were, and how scared they had become. Their lives were difficult, he explained, because they had to treat people who were like them as if they had a disease. They were scared, he said, because if they revealed that they themselves were queer, they would lose their jobs.

Fryer raised his voice, and forced the psychiatric profession to confront some awkward truths about how they were treating queer people. Regardless of whether or not individual psychiatrists agreed with him, he had started a conversation that no one else had dared to, and even in disguise made himself visible to other queer people. He spoke his truth, and the mainstream, straight world had to acknowledge it.

One year after Fryer's speech, at the next annual convention of the APA in 1973, members were asked to vote on whether homosexuality should be considered a mental disorder. It was decided, by a significant majority, that it should not, and it was removed from the APA's book of mental illnesses.

Fryer's speech was a major turning point for the queer community; not only did it send shockwaves through the medical world, it also started to profoundly change the way people spoke and thought about queerness.

> **At the time Fryer stood up to make his announcement, homosexuality was officially listed in The American Psychiatric Association's book of mental illnesses**

A Community in Crisis

Despite the work of Fryer and other activists like him, the belief that something was "wrong" with queer people was very deeply rooted, and many cultures around the world continued to associate queerness with disease.

This meant that when members of the queer community started to become ill from a genuine disease, society was very slow to offer help.

It's not known exactly when this new disease appeared in the USA, but in the early 1970s it began to spread through the population. It had reached epidemic proportions in parts of colonial Africa before spreading to other parts of the world. The disease attacked people's immune systems, leaving them vulnerable to infections that the body would normally fight off; doctors had never seen anything like it before. It took a long time for the disease to be named but we now know it as HIV, the Human Immunodeficiency Virus.

It was a terrifying time for the queer community; people were losing their friends and partners to a disease that no one understood, and which no one could treat

Today many treatments exist that can block the transmission of HIV, and keep people who have it healthy. Those treatments are mostly available in wealthy countries, though, and the virus is still a very serious health problem in poorer parts of the world. Left untreated, HIV develops into a life-threatening condition called AIDS. When it first appeared, no one knew enough about it to understand how to treat the virus, so people began dying in large numbers.

HIV became an epidemic in the USA and Europe in the 80s and 90s. While anyone can get HIV, gay men and trans people were particularly vulnerable to infection, and many began to get seriously ill and die. It was a terrifying time for the queer community; people were losing their friends and partners to a disease that no one understood, and which no one could treat.

> The queer community had no option but to try and look after itself, to offer support, love, and compassion where it could

As medical science slowly started to develop ways to treat HIV, the queer community looked to their doctors and politicians to make drugs available, to tell them what advances were being made, to give them hope. But the ongoing prejudice they faced meant that very few people were willing to help. The prevailing attitude was that queer people deserved what they were experiencing. Because of this, many HIV sufferers felt they had to hide their illness, and those who were diagnosed often couldn't count on much help and support from their doctors.

The queer community had no option but to try and look after itself, to offer support, love, and compassion where it could. Because so many gay men were ill, queer women and lesbians in particular began taking care of their male friends. It was a difficult, lonely experience for many, but it started to bring the community together in a way that hadn't been seen before, and was ultimately to lead to a whole new wave of activism.

Although today's treatments can help people with HIV live long, healthy lives, the queer community still remembers the time when so many died. In the early 90s, a group of artists in New York launched the Red Ribbon Project, an initiative to honor the memory of those who lost their lives to HIV, and show compassion for people currently living with the disease. Red ribbons are often worn on World AIDS Day, a yearly global event held to offer solidarity and support for anyone affected by HIV.

The New York Ballroom Scene

Although Harvey Milk's message about coming out had embedded itself in queer America, and more and more people were finding the courage to step forward and tell their friends and family who they were, this was still very risky and the consequences could be devastating ...

M

any young people were disowned by their families when they came out. They had to face a world that didn't understand them and didn't want to make space for them ...

Unsure where to go, they were often drawn to larger cities with established queer communities, such as San Francisco, Chicago, and New York, where they could meet others in similar situations and find people who would help or take care of them. Building a supportive and inclusive community was particularly important for black and Hispanic people, who were especially discriminated against because of their skin color as well as their sexuality.

In New York during the 60s and 70s, a new underground movement

In New York, a new underground movement started to emerge as displaced queer people began to band together into groups known as "houses"

started to emerge as displaced queer people began to band together into groups known as "houses." The houses were part street gang, part surrogate family, and each one was named after its legendary queer founder, who acted as "mother" or "father" of the house. Well-known drag queen Crystal LaBeija became Mother of the House of Labeija, while Hector Xtravaganza founded the House of Xtravaganza. The mothers and fathers were responsible for looking after the house members, who were known as the "children." Children would take on the name of the house as their surname, to show that they belonged. In a world where many queer people had become estranged from their original families, the houses became extremely important; members of a house would look after each other, and make sure everyone was safe and well.

The children of the houses would meet at regular events called Balls, where they would walk like models, competing in different categories. While they walked they would "serve looks," showing off their ability to emulate glamorous women, soldiers, or business executives. Drag queens, butch women, feminine men ... no matter the category, each contestant tried to be more fabulous and impressive than the last. The ability to look authentic, to appear as if you truly owned the character you were creating, was called "realness," and became the most important aspect of any ball. People who served realness would receive high scores from the judges—ten out of ten across the board! Those whose outfits were lacking, or who didn't behave well, would be judged poorly, and have their style picked apart by the crowd. Winners would receive trophies, and respect.

> **Although the competition was intense, Balls were always exciting, glamorous, and fun**

Some competitions involved a new style of dance called voguing, where dancers flowed between poses, like pictures in the fashion magazine *Vogue*. It was full of attitude and control, and no one had seen anything like it before. Gradually, voguing became popular outside the Ballrooms in the worlds of fashion and music. One of the most skilled voguers was Willi Ninja, mother of the House of Ninja, who became famous as a dancer and a model outside of the Ballroom scene, as well as within it.

Although the competition was intense, Balls were always exciting, glamorous, and fun; they were places where people were free to be whatever gender they chose, and to wear whatever they wanted, just so long as they looked fabulous! The children of the Ballroom scene became legendary and are still known for being fierce and proud. The Ballrooms and runways of New York became glittering moments of triumph for queer people, places where they truly felt they belonged.

"Something Beautiful"
Gilbert Baker

Voguing wasn't the only new thing to come out of the New York Ballroom scene. The Ballroom community taught queer people how to be strong and fierce, and provided them with surrogate families who would support them, but it had wider effects too …

The way people spoke, moved, and thought about themselves in the Ballrooms had a ripple effect across the queer community and began to establish a culture that was unique to queer people.

Gilbert Baker, an activist and artist, wanted to design a symbol that the queer community could rally around

This was important: for many years queer people had been staying quiet, keeping their heads down so that they could exist within mainstream society. Now, in the radical post-Stonewall world, they began to realize that the key to their liberation lay in making themselves visible—in grouping together and shouting with one voice. The creation of a shared culture and a shared history gave queer people something to group together around, and an identity which was theirs alone. Connecting to this new culture started to become a rite of passage for those who had recently come out.

On the other side of the country in San Francisco, another equally important element of queer culture was established, one that would come to symbolize hope and freedom for LGBTQ+ people everywhere.

Gilbert Baker, an activist and artist, wanted to design a symbol that the queer community could rally around. For years, activist groups had been using the pink triangle as an emblem of identity and resistance, but Baker felt its associations with the Nazis made it too negative. He wanted something that could take the community into the future, full of hope and joy— something that belonged only to queer people, not to their enemies.

So Baker designed a flag that he believed was a truly positive and inclusive representation of the LGBTQ+ community, and, on June 25, 1978 at the annual Gay Freedom Day Parade, it was unveiled. Held up against the bright blue sky, the flag was striped with beautiful, vivid colors: a dazzling rainbow.

The different colored stripes represent the diversity of the queer community, while the rainbow itself is a symbol of nature. The flag was the first emblem that the queer community had made for itself, and people felt proud of it, and proud to stand beneath it. "Pride" soon became a name for the movement Stonewall had begun, and the rainbow flag became its symbol.

> Held up against the bright blue sky, the flag was striped with beautiful, vivid colors: a dazzling rainbow

The design of the flag has changed occasionally over the years and from place to place. In 2017 a new version of the flag, with black and brown stripes added to represent non-white people in Pride, was unveiled at the Philadelphia Pride march. Today, alongside the rainbow flag, you can see many other flags representing different groups in the queer community, and the specific challenges and prejudices they face. There are flags for the bisexual, intersex, and asexual communities, there is a specific flag for the trans community, and for many, many others. Most are based on the layout of the rainbow flag, with their own unique colors or design included.

Over the years, the rainbow flag has become a symbol of freedom, hope, and friendship for lesbian, gay, bisexual, and trans people, and is a powerful image of resistance in parts of the world where being queer is still dangerous or illegal. Used to mark spaces as being safe for queer people, the rainbow flag is hung over buildings, bars, and other meeting places. You may also see people wearing the rainbow flag as a badge, signaling that they are queer, or an ally (friend) of the queer community.

Wherever the flag is flying, it represents hope for the future and connection to the past: a symbol of community and togetherness.

Pride Around the World.

Gradually Pride developed into a massive global movement as more and more people chose to get involved. Now, every year, in all sorts of places around the world, queer communities come together in events which are equal part celebration, commemoration, and protest.

Known as "Prides," these are moments when the queer community can remember its history and push forward into the future.

Prides often take the form of large, colorful street parties, generally focused around a parade or march. The rainbow flag flies everywhere during a Pride and is often a key feature of the march itself.

As well as being a lot of fun, Pride events are a modern expression of that idea which has run through queer activism since Ulrichs stood up and made his speech; the same idea that drove the Mattachines to stage their sip-in and that made Milk and Lorde speak so eloquently about the need to come out: the key to queer liberation is visibility. Prides are moments when the queer community makes itself known to the mainstream community around it. The color and noise of a Pride and its parade are impossible to ignore. It makes queer people safe *because* it makes them visible, and it gives each individual

The color and noise of a Pride and its parade are impossible to ignore

a place to express their identity on their own terms, while celebrating queer culture and remembering queer history.

The first Pride events took place in the USA in the years following Stonewall, but the idea quickly caught on elsewhere, and LGBTQ+ communities around the world began organizing their own marches and celebrations to connect to global queer movements.

In Australia, one of the largest Pride events takes place every year in Sydney: the Mardi Gras. In 1978, a protest for gay rights was violently broken up by Sydney police, who arrested and imprisoned many people. Echoing what had happened at Stonewall, many felt that the police had acted aggressively and treated the protesters unfairly. Over the months that followed, a series of protests about the way the police had behaved forced a change in laws, allowing queer people to be more open in public. One year later, 3,000 people marched through Sydney to mark the event and celebrate the changes. In 1980, a street party was organized alongside the march. This became the Mardi Gras, which is now one of the most popular Prides in the world. It not only celebrates the global queer movement, but also connects to local history for the Australian queer community.

The biggest Pride in the world is in São Paulo, Brazil, which regularly hosts more than 3 million people

Along with Sydney's Mardi Gras, some of the largest Prides take place in Madrid, Spain; New York, USA; London, UK; and Amsterdam, Netherlands. The biggest Pride in the world is in São Paulo, Brazil, which regularly hosts more than 3 million people. There are also well established Prides in Cologne, Germany; San Francisco, USA; and Tel Aviv, Israel. The first African Pride took place in Johannesburg, South Africa in 1990.

While Prides are open to all, there are other events which celebrate the identity of particular strands of the queer community. These celebrations, like Black Pride or the Trans Pride march, are moments of visibility for groups who often feel marginalized within the larger queer community, as well as within mainstream culture. They ensure that everyone is recognized and celebrated, and acknowledge the diversity that exists in the movement as a whole.

In some parts of the world, public celebrations are difficult because there are laws against being queer, or because queer people live under the threat of violence. In other places, Prides are smaller-scale events. But wherever they happen, and however big or small, they are beacons of hope for queer people everywhere.

Trans Struggles;
Trans Rights

One of the largest celebrations of trans identity takes place every year during San Francisco Pride weekend. The San Francisco Trans March was first organized in 2004, after an anonymous email was sent to various queer activists in the city, calling for trans, non-binary, and gender-variant people in the area to meet and march through San Francisco. The email explained that the main aim of the march was to make the trans community visible. It ended with the following words:

Dress up, show up, bring signs, speak out, and be what happens!

The call was circulated, and people came. The first march was made up of a few hundred people, and numbers grew and grew in the following years.

People who identify as a different gender from the one they are given at birth have existed throughout history and across different cultures. Gender norms can be very rigid; people are often expected to behave in a particular way according to their gender and can be treated very badly if they don't. Trans, intersex, and non-binary people encounter serious discrimination in many parts of the world, and can face constant threats of violence and aggression from the societies in which they live. Trans people can also end up having to fight serious legal battles to have their true gender recognized, and to gain access to services or spaces that are often more easily available to everyone else.

Back in 1920s Berlin, Magnus Hirschfeld was championing the cause of trans people alongside his activism for other queer people. Hirschfeld understood that men and women could think about their gender very differently to the way society expected, and offered support and advice to people who struggled with those expectations. In 1930, he met the Danish artist and model Lili Elbe, whose life is portrayed in the bestselling novel *The Danish Girl*. Elbe had been assigned male at birth but had been living as a woman since her early 20s, and had traveled to Germany to undergo gender confirmation surgery, becoming one of the first people to receive this sort of treatment. Sadly, in

1931, Elbe died as a result of her surgeries, which were not well understood at the time, but she wrote that she had lived "a whole and happy human life" as a consequence of being able to express her gender identity and live as a woman.

Today the process by which someone becomes recognized as the gender they identify with, rather than the gender they were given at birth, is called "transitioning." There are many ways to transition, and lots of them don't involve any surgery at all. Nevertheless, access to medical services that help with transitioning has been a major part of the trans struggle for a long time.

Elbe's story was not well known outside Germany and Denmark, and many records of her existence had been destroyed when the Nazis shut down and vandalized Hirschfeld's institute in 1933. But after World War II, the American and British public started to become more aware of trans individuals, when Christine Jorgensen in the US, and Roberta Cowell and Michael Dillon in the UK, became some of the first people to undergo newly developed surgical gender confirmations. These were the earliest stories about being trans that many people had heard, and they paved the way for the trans movement that followed.

In 1966, three years before Stonewall, a group of trans people began a demonstration at Compton's Cafeteria in San Francisco. The cafe

In 1966, three years before Stonewall, a group of trans people began a demonstration at Compton's Cafeteria in San Francisco

was a meeting spot for the trans community, and, like Stonewall, had been the target of aggressive police raids. The demonstration became the Compton's Cafeteria Riot, which kickstarted trans activism in the city.

To this day, trans people continue to fight hard for rights. In 1972, Sweden became the first country to allow people to legally change their gender, although they were required to undergo various medical treatments in order to do so. The first European country to allow someone to correct their gender without any medical intervention was Denmark in 2014.

In 1986, Lou Sullivan, a founder of the Gay and Lesbian Historical Society, set up FTM (Female to Male) International, one of the first activist groups specifically for trans men in San Francisco. Sullivan was a passionate writer and public speaker and campaigned to have trans men recognized by the medical profession.

In 1998, Rita Hester, a black trans woman, was murdered in Allston, Massachusetts. Her death sparked outrage in the trans community and led to the birth of International Transgender Day of Remembrance, held every year on November 20 to commemorate those who have lost their lives because of intolerance and prejudice. Names like Brandon Teena, Gwen Araujo, Venus Xtravaganza, and Amanda Milan are remembered among many, many others.

Finding ways to represent queer people as a single community, while also acknowledging all the different queer identities that exist, has always been a challenge. The rainbow flag was designed to belong to the queer community as a whole, but the various groups it encompasses have fought hard for individual recognition.

The word queer comprises many identities: gay, lesbian, ace, bi, pan, poly, trans, non-binary, genderqueer … there is a vast and growing diversity of names and groups within the queer community, reflecting the fact that there are many ways of not being straight.

But having an array of potential labels to choose from is a very recent development, and the result of a long struggle for a positive and inclusive vocabulary.

The word "homosexual" is often associated with the Hungarian journalist and early queer activist Karl-Maria Kertbeny. Born in Austria in the 1820s, Kertbeny moved to Berlin in 1868. There he began corresponding with Karl Ulrichs on the topic of same-gender attraction. One of those letters contains the earliest use of the word "homosexuality" (or *homosexualität* in German),

By taking ownership of the name and calling themselves gay, they made the word into something more positive

which Kertbeny used to describe men who were attracted to other men. Like Ulrichs, Kertbeny argued passionately against the way European cultures treated queer people, and wrote a series of pamphlets on the topic. He argued that people were born being attracted to a particular gender, and tried to convince society that queer men were not damaged or unwell in any way.

"Homosexuality" found its way into the English language and caught on as a way to refer to queerness, but it took on a much less positive meaning than Kertbeny had intended. Victorian society, as we know, believed that being attracted to "opposite sex" people was the natural, healthy condition, and viewed queerness as unhealthy or dirty. They used the word homosexuality as a name for that disease. For a long time after that, homosexuality was a medical diagnosis and, later, a crime.

Around the 1940s, the word "gay" started to mean "men who are attracted to men." Initially it was used as an insult and an accusation, intended to keep gay men in their place by making them feel ashamed and scared.

But gradually, queer men started to use the name to describe themselves and their community, which changed things. Because there was now a name for the community, it became more visible. Gay men could find each other and form friendships and relationships. By taking ownership of the name and calling themselves gay, they made the word into something more positive.

Although many queer women use it to describe themselves, the word gay has always been strongly associated with men. In the 60s and 70s, queer women began to push their own identities forward, and started to describe themselves as lesbians. The word lesbian comes from the name of a Greek island, Lesbos. In the sixth century BCE, Lesbos was home to the poet Sappho, whose writings speak of love between

Lesbos was home to the poet Sappho, whose writings speak of love between women

women. Although this sounds quite positive, the name was also used by the Victorians to describe women they thought were ill. Again, queer women took that name and turned it into an identity, making themselves more powerful in the process.

Gradually, the phrase "gay and lesbian" started to be used to refer to all queer people.

This, though, was a problem for those who didn't easily identify as either. Bisexual and trans people in particular felt ignored and marginalized, and campaigned for their own recognition. Bisexual activists such as Maggi Rubenstein, and trans activists like Susan Stryker, fought hard to have their communities acknowledged by other queer people. The devastating effects of HIV forced different groups to come together in mutual support, and in the 1990s the queer community started to be known as GLBT, for Gay, Lesbian, Bisexual, and Trans.

Today it is most commonly written as LGBT. Often the letter Q is added to the end, which stands for queer, or sometimes for questioning. There are still communities fighting for their recognition within the queer movement, and their initials are sometimes added to the acronym: I for intersex, A for asexual, U for undecided. Increasingly, a plus sign is added to make it clear that the community is open to and accepting of anyone who feels as if they belong: LGBTQ+.

ACT UP

On May 21, 1990, activists from across America descended on the National Institutes of Health's campus in Bethesda, Maryland, USA. Their aim was to protest against the Institutes' response to the continuing AIDS crisis, and to draw attention to the way the US government and medical institutions were treating all the communities affected by HIV.

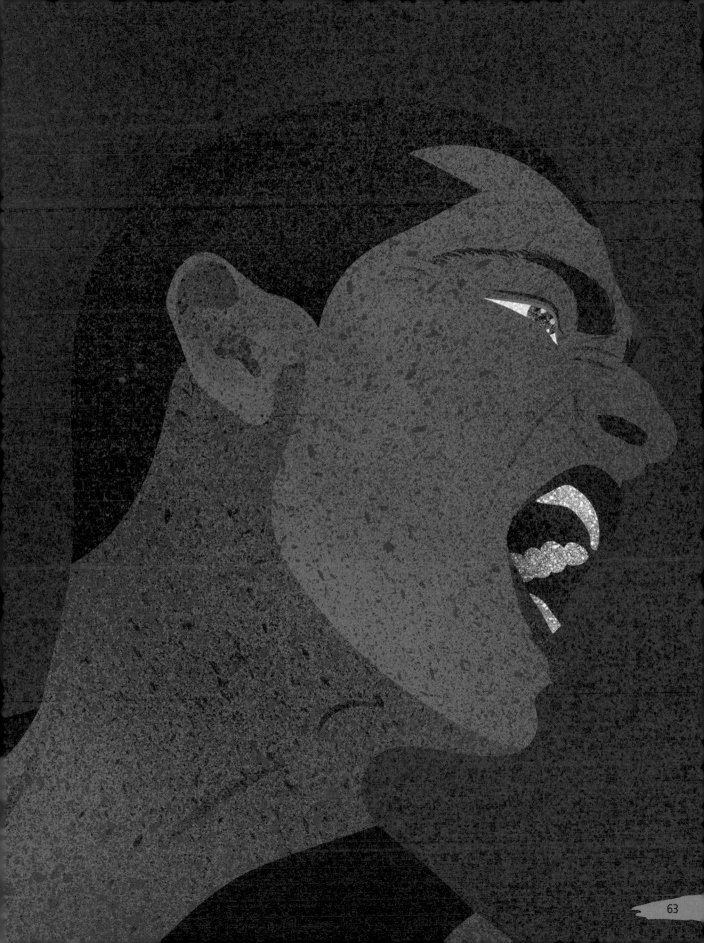

The protest, which involved well over one thousand people, was loud, theatrical, and full of anger. Some people performed political skits on improvised stages, others lit fires and burned images of the NIH's director.

At one point a group of 20 or so activists ran into the building and occupied the office of one of the Institutes' senior medical staff. Protesters chanted and sang; the atmosphere was charged.

Among those gathered, one symbol could be seen emblazoned on clothes and placards: an inverted pink triangle against a black background. At one point a huge banner was unfurled by the crowd. All in black, with white lettering, the banner spelled out its simple message to everyone watching: SILENCE = DEATH.

> Protesters chanted and sang; the atmosphere was charged

This was the activist group ACT UP (AIDS Coalition to Unleash Power), which had formed three years previously in response to the way the US government had handled the AIDS crisis.

While Pride had been gaining global momentum throughout the 70s and 80s, queer people were nevertheless still facing injustice and prejudice on a daily basis, and the HIV epidemic was getting worse. By the time of the protest, thousands of people had died from HIV, and many more were seriously ill.

Queer communities in various parts of the world felt as if their governments weren't doing enough to help them fight the disease. In the USA, the government was very slow to publicly acknowledge the scale of the epidemic. There was little research into HIV being carried out, and no communication from the government to the communities most affected by it. The research that *was* being done excluded the very groups who were most affected by the illness: gay, bisexual, and trans people, black people, women, and children. The companies conducting the research were moving slowly, and kept telling people to be patient, that research took time—but people with HIV didn't have time to spare: all around the queer community people were sick and dying.

In 1987 New York, author and playwright Larry Kramer founded a new queer activist group specifically focused on drawing attention to the lack of response to the epidemic. ACT UP was a radical protest organization, whose main aim was raising awareness about the AIDS crisis, both inside and outside the queer community. Its members took part in a series of organized protests and non-violent acts of civil disobedience, often very loud and theatrical, to let the world know that people were dying.

ACT UP was a radical protest organization, whose main aim was raising awareness about the AIDS crisis, both inside and outside the queer community

ACT UP members would chain themselves to public buildings to block access, or organize marches carrying photographs of people who had died of AIDS. They would disrupt television broadcasts, all to raise the profile of the epidemic, and the people it was affecting.

Other members of ACT UP learned as much about biology and biochemistry as they could, so that they could talk directly to scientists developing drugs for HIV, and fight back against ignorance and prejudice. Chapters of the organization began to open up in other cities: Paris, France, in 1989, and Sydney, Australia, in 1990. Its founding principle was that queer people had to stand up and make themselves heard, because their lives were at risk if they stayed quiet. This was the idea behind their "SILENCE = DEATH" motto.

Their strategy worked. As a result of the 1990 protest, HIV research was redesigned to specifically include the communities most affected by it, and ACT UP members were appointed to committees where important decisions about research were being made. The queer community became properly integrated into the government's response to HIV, and at long last real progress became possible for the first time.

Section 28

In 1988, the British government voted in a law known as Section 28, which made it illegal for schools to talk positively about homosexuality. This meant it was impossible for schools to provide their students with information about safe sex or LGBTQ+ communities, and made many young queer people feel isolated and lonely. Under this law, books like the one you are holding now would not have been allowed in British schools

Homosexuality" had been illegal in Britain for hundreds of years. Although this affected people of all genders, only men were specifically mentioned by law because British society didn't acknowledge that women could be queer.

The mere notion that Wilde and Douglas might be having a sexual relationship was enough for British society to be outraged, and for the courts to take an interest

In 1895, the famous playwright and author Oscar Wilde became involved in a court case over his relationship with the poet Lord Alfred Douglas. The two men had met a few years previously and had begun an affair, which enraged Douglas's father. The mere notion that Wilde and Douglas might be having a sexual relationship was enough for British society to be outraged, and for the courts to take an interest. As a result of the trial, Wilde spent two years in prison, enduring horrendous conditions and a public humiliation from which he never recovered.

The laws against homosexuality remained in place until well into the twentieth century, but a series of high profile prosecutions of gay men in the 1950s forced the British parliament to start reconsidering them. In 1952, the mathematician and World War II codebreaker Alan Turing was arrested and tried for "gross indecency" because the police discovered he had been in a relationship with another man. Turing was convicted, and given two options for his sentence: go to prison or agree to medical treatment for his queerness. Turing chose the treatment, which was designed to remove his sexual desire completely. Like Wilde, and many others who had similar experiences with the Britsh courts, Turing was never the same afterward. He died in 1954, after poisoning himself with cyanide.

Turing's court case, alongside those of other men in the public eye at the time, such as the journalist and writer Peter Wildeblood and the aristocrat Lord Edward Montagu, forced British society to properly acknowledge that queer people existed, and to consider the way they were treated by the country's laws. After much debate, sex between men became legal in 1967 in England and Wales, 1980 in Scotland and 1982 in Northern Ireland.

These were important milestones for queer people in the UK, but they only decriminalized "private acts" of homosexuality. Men who kissed or held hands with other men in public, or behaved in ways that were considered visibly queer, could still be arrested for "public indecency." Additionally,

> In 1952, the mathematician and World War II codebreaker Alan Turing was arrested and tried for "gross indecency" because the police found out he had been in a relationship with another man

laws like Section 28 could be fairly easily brought in, and queer people would have whole new legal challenges to contend with.

In 1989, in response to Section 28, some high-profile British activists formed a group to campaign for lesbian and gay equality. The group, which pushed for open conversation with the UK government, named itself after the riots that had kickstarted the queer movement twenty years before: Stonewall.

The following year, another queer activist group emerged in the UK. In many ways similar to ACT UP, OutRage! engaged in non-violent civil disobedience in order to push for equal rights for queer people. The tactics used by the two groups were different, but they had the same broad aim: to end homophobia.

As a result of pressure from these groups, Section 28 was finally removed from British law in 2003, and the laws that had been used to arrest and convict gay men were fully overturned in 2013. Although OutRage! dissolved in 2011, Stonewall still exists in the UK, and has become a very successful lobbying organization for LGBTQ+ rights. Among its various triumphs have been its campaigns for the equalization of age of consent for queer people, to have laws put in place to allow same-sex couples to adopt, and, most recently, for marriage equality in the UK.

Landmark Moments

The UK was by no means the first country to legalize sex between two same-gender people. A number of countries, including France, Belgium, the Netherlands, Japan, and Brazil, had changed their laws as early as the eighteenth and nineteenth centuries. Others took longer … in Australia, for example, homosexuality wasn't legal throughout the whole country until 1997, the same year as China.

Sadly, in many parts of the world, homosexuality remains illegal, often as a consequence of laws brought in by colonizing European powers.

For many thousands of years, India accepted and celebrated diversity in both gender and sexuality. Ancient Indian mythology is full of loving and sexual relationships between same-gender gods or heroes, and the notion that people might not be either male or female was so common that third gender individuals were well recognized in Indian society.

All that changed in 1861, when the colonial British government outlawed homosexuality in what became known as Section 377 of the Indian Constitution. That law remained in force until 2018 when, after more than 20 hard years of protest and activism from Indian LGBTQ+ groups, the Indian Supreme Court ruled that homosexuality should no longer be considered a crime. In their historic ruling, the judges drew upon the idea of the rainbow and its many colors as a natural symbol of queer liberation: "We must realise that different hues and colors together make the painting of humanity beautiful and this beauty is the essence of humanity."

"We must realize that different hues and colors together make the painting of humanity beautiful and this beauty is the essence of humanity"

Elsewhere, former colonies still have laws inherited from European countries which outlaw homosexuality. Zambia, for example, has kept the anti-queer laws that the British colonial government introduced in the 1800s, and Jamaican laws prohibiting sex between two men have existed since 1864, having also been brought to the country by colonial Britain. Just as in the UK when these laws were created, there is no mention of queer women because their existence isn't acknowledged—their identities remain sidelined and overlooked. Despite the ongoing work of activist groups like J-FLAG (the Jamaican Forum for Lesbians, All-Sexuals and Gays), life for queer people is extremely difficult in Jamaica, and they can face serious discrimination and violence on a daily basis.

In other countries, such as Saudi Arabia and Russia, laws against LGBTQ+ people are so fiercely enforced that merely forming an activist group can be considered a crime. Although homosexuality has been legal in Russia since 1993, sweeping laws against the promotion of homosexuality were introduced in 2013. These laws have been used to arrest and imprison many people and have resulted in a sharp rise in homophobic violence in the country. They also apply in all of Russia's republics. In 2017, Chechnya saw a violent crackdown against queer Chechen citizens that has led to an unknown number of gay men being imprisoned— and possibly killed.

In the USA, laws are very complex, and can vary from state to state. Sexual activity between same-sex adults was made legal across the country in 2003, after the arrest, trial and subsequent conviction of John Lawrence Jr., and Tyron Garner for homosexual conduct in Texas. After making an appeal, Lawrence and Garner's case was reviewed by the American Supreme Court, which ruled that the government had no right to interfere in private, consensual sex between American citizens.

But there are many important legal battles still to be won and laws in the USA can change very quickly. The State of California, for example, had begun issuing marriage licenses to same-gender couples in June 2008, only to have the laws that supported them overturned in November of the same year. Eventually, in 2013 the Supreme Court intervened to restore marriage rights to gay and lesbian couples in California, and these are still in place today. And although same-sex marriage was legalized across the USA in 2015, after many years of powerful activism and campaigning, the recognition that queer couples receive can still vary enormously from state to state.

In 2015, the same year that marriage equality became legal nationwide, US President Barack Obama addressed the entire country in the annual State of the Union speech. During this, he said the following words: "we defend free speech ... and condemn the persecution of women, or religious minorities, or people who are lesbian, gay, bisexual, or transgender."

It was a truly historic moment. This was the first time a US president had used the words lesbian, bisexual, or transgender in the State of the Union speech, the first time that the LGBT community as a whole had been officially recognized in this context, and the first time that a president had called to end the persecution of queer people in the USA. For the queer community in the USA, and elsewhere around the world, this signaled that the lives and happiness of LGBTQ+ people were finally being taken seriously at the highest levels of government in one of the most powerful countries in the world.

> In 2015, the same year that marriage equality became legal nationwide, US President Barack Obama addressed the entire country in the annual State of the Union speech

Equality For All!

On April 17, 2013, the speaker of the New Zealand Parliament announced the results of a vote that would allow same-gender couples to get married. It passed, and the politicians who had argued for it took a moment to congratulate each other while the people watching clapped and cheered.

As the applause died down, a single voice rose up from the public gallery, singing a Māori love song, Pōkarekare Ana. Everyone joined in, and suddenly the whole room was singing in celebration.

For a long time, even in countries where homosexuality is legal, same-gender couples have not been allowed to get married, despite the fact that the freedom to marry whoever you want to is listed by the United Nations in the Universal Declaration of Human Rights:

Those who argue against the idea of queer people marrying tend to think of marriage as something that only exists between a man and a woman

Article 16.
(1) Men and women of full age, without any limitation due to race, nationality or religion, have the right to marry and to found a family.

Queer people in many countries have fought hard to win the sort of recognition for their relationships that straight couples have, often in the face of some very serious opposition. Those who argue against the idea of queer people marrying tend to think of marriage as something that only exists between a man and a woman, and argue that changing marriage laws would lead to destructive new ideas about what constitutes a family.

But for queer people, and for all the queer activists around the world who campaigned and still campaign for marriage equality, restricting marriage to straight people is discrimination. It connects to the long history of viewing queerness as undesirable and inferior.

In 2017, Penny Wong, the first openly LGBTQ+ female senator in Australia, put it like this: "For LGBTIQ Australians, the message conveyed by the discrimination in our nation's marriage laws has been clear. It is a message that we are lesser. It is a message that we are less valued as citizens. It is a message that our relationships and our children matter less. And it is a message that, because of who we love, our love is worth less."

There are still many places around the world where marriage is restricted to heterosexual couples only, but the twenty-first century saw some important changes made in many countries.

The Netherlands became the first country in the world to grant full marriage equality in 2000. A year later, when the laws properly came into effect, four gay couples were married by the Mayor of Amsterdam in front of a crowd of friends, family, and politicians. The crowd cheered and applauded as the newly married couples, three made up of men, one of women, kissed and hugged, celebrating their newly recognized relationship and their new equality.

Many other countries followed: Belgium, Canada, Spain, and South Africa all legalized same-sex marriages in the next five years. Marriage has been available to same-sex couples in the UK, except for Northern Ireland, since 2014, and has been upheld as a civil right for queer American citizens since 2015. The Republic of Ireland brought in full marriage equality in 2015. By an overwhelming majority, Australia voted in favor of marriage equality in 2017, which is when Penny Wong gave her rousing speech.

But although legalizing same-sex marriage is an important step toward liberation for some, other kinds of queer relationship continue to struggle for recognition. LGBTQ+ parents, and trans parents in particular, still face prejudice and discrimination when they try to raise a family. Many others feel as if traditional ideas of marriage just don't apply to their relationships, and are left feeling frustrated and excluded when their partners and families aren't accepted or celebrated.

The queer rights movement has come a long way since Stonewall, and the number of countries that now grant queer people the freedom to marry represents a major victory for the LGBTQ+ community. But it's by no means the end of the story …

> The crowd cheered and applauded as the newly married couples, three made up of men, one of women, kissed and hugged

Whether or not they're married, queer people can often run into real difficulties when they decide to have children. Many countries are structured around an idea that only men and women can reproduce, and strongly resist the possibility that same-sex couples or trans people might also be able to become parents.

Proud
Parents

n 2008, trans man Thomas Beatie announced to the world that he was pregnant, becoming one of the first men to carry a child. Beatie and his wife Nancy lived in Oregon, USA, and had been married for five years before announcing the pregnancy.

The couple had planned to have children since their marriage, but Nancy was unable to conceive so they decided that Thomas would carry their child.

Thomas Beatie decided to make his story public, to help raise awareness of families like his, and the difficulties they can face when they try to build a life for themselves

Thomas decided to make his story public, to help raise awareness of families like his and the difficulties they can face when they try to build a life for themselves. Thanks to his decision, we know a great deal about his life and the kinds of issues he and his wife faced as a consequence of trying to have children.

Thomas self-identified as male at the age of ten, having been assigned a female gender at birth. He began transitioning in his early 20s, and in 2002 had surgery to reshape his chest so that it looked more traditionally masculine. Like many, but not all, trans men, Thomas opted not to have any surgery on his lower body, and kept the reproductive body parts he had been born with.

Thomas stopped taking testosterone, which allowed his body to resume its menstrual cycle, and became pregnant using sperm from a donor. Fairly quickly, the couple began experiencing problems as a consequence of Thomas's trans identity. Doctors and nurses would refuse to provide him care or advice, would refuse to address Thomas as "he" or recognize the couple's marriage. Receptionists at clinics would laugh at them; even friends and family stopped supporting them.

Despite all the difficulties, Thomas gave birth to the Beaties' first child in 2008, and later to two more children. Other trans men have since gone public with their own stories. In Canada, Trevor MacDonald wrote publicly about the difficulties he faced while trying to breastfeed his children in 2016. A year later, Hayden Cross and Scott Parker became the first men in the UK to publicly announce their pregnancies. These stories directly challenge the way many cultures view masculinity, reproduction, fatherhood, and motherhood, and open up new ways of thinking about how families might work.

> South Africa is the only African country where same-gender couples can adopt children, having been given the right to do so in 2002

While individual LGBTQ+ people have often been able to adopt children as single parents, same-gender couples have only fairly recently been allowed to jointly adopt children, and even then only in 26 countries worldwide. South Africa is the only African country where same-gender couples can adopt children, having been given the right to do so in 2002. In the USA, adoption rights for gay and lesbian couples were granted nationwide in 2017. Joint adoption is available to same-gender couples in most European countries, with the Netherlands being the first to change its law in 2001. Australia began allowing joint adoption for gay and lesbian couples in all territories in 2018. But even where laws exist to permit adoption, queer families often experience extremely high levels of prejudice and discrimination from society as a whole.

Queer couples who, like the Beaties, want to have children without adopting, face a whole other set of challenges, since fertility services are often very strongly skewed toward heterosexual couples. The option of having a child through surrogacy, or sperm or egg donation, often needs to be worked out very carefully to protect all individuals concerned because laws aren't fully set up to accommodate them.

Fierce and Fabulous!

Legal battles are very important, but the struggle for queer liberation doesn't just involve changing laws. Homophobia and transphobia are still major problems and present huge barriers for queer people, even in countries where considerable progress has been made. Attitudes around the world need to shift to accept that queer people exist—and that they have a right to be happy.

LGBTQ+ people have been fighting for these changes for many, many years. Along the way, they've created their own culture where they can connect with each other and feel welcome.

Queer culture is loud, proud, fierce, and fabulous, and is built around the idea that people who don't fit in to the mainstream, straight world should have their own places to express themselves however they want to. Like the runways of the New York Ballroom scene, these spaces can produce new ways of moving, dressing, and dancing—new traditions that belong to the community itself.

Occasionally those traditions spill out of queer culture to become part of the mainstream world. The glamor and flair of the runways, and voguing itself, became extremely popular, and were picked up by mainstream pop stars and musicians. In the 80s and 90s, pop legends like Grace Jones and Madonna purposefully made queer culture part of their

Pop legends like Grace Jones and Madonna purposefully made queer culture part of their performance, just like Lady Gaga in the early 2000s

performance, just like Lady Gaga in the early 2000s. Their bold, striking dance moves and larger-than-life, spectacular outfits and looks carried the playfulness and joy of queerness into the mainstream. The modern pop scene is full of popstars being authentic, fierce, and proud in the music they produce. Whether they know it or not, they are carrying forward the legacy of queer culture.

We've already seen how the artists Stein, Gluck, and Kahlo became key figures in artistic and social movements, and icons in their own right. There have been many other queer people in the arts whose work has had a major impact on mainstream culture too, like the artist and film-maker Andy Warhol; photographers such as Robert Mapplethorpe and Nan Goldin; writers such as Sarah Waters, James Baldwin, and Radclyffe Hall; and musicians such as Freddie Mercury, Lou Reed, and Frank Ocean. Whether singers, dancers, photographers, or writers, queer artists and performers all bring new, playful and energetic ideas to their work. All of these people and others have played a huge part in shaping the recent history of art, literature, and music, and have, in their own ways, brought queer culture out into the wider world.

Yet while queerness was becoming a powerful driver of art and pop culture, it took some time for mainstream society to accept open depictions of LGBTQ+ lives in film and television. The UK's first gay kiss was broadcast in 1974 in a half-hour drama called *Girl* that told a story of two female soldiers falling in love. It was aired late at night, so children wouldn't watch it, and was preceded by a special announcement from the BBC, warning people of what they were about to see. It took until 1987 for a prime-time UK TV show to broadcast a gay kiss, when the soap opera *Eastenders* aired a brief moment of intimacy between two male characters. Mainstream British culture at the time was full of homophobia and prejudice, and the kiss caused such outrage that its impact was even debated by politicians in Parliament.

Slowly, however, attitudes changed. In 1991 the US legal drama *LA Law* became the first American TV show to air a same-gender kiss, between two women, while the teen drama *Dawson's Creek* is widely renowned for airing the first passionate kiss between two gay male characters in 2000. Other shows, such as *My So-Called Life* and *Buffy the Vampire Slayer*, broke new ground in their portrayal of gay and lesbian relationships. Eventually, shows that focused on queer people and queer lives began to emerge—*Will and Grace*, *The L Word*, the UK's trailblazing drama *Queer as Folk*. These shows became important cultural milestones in the fight for recognition.

> Other shows, such as *My So-Called Life* and *Buffy the Vampire Slayer*, broke new ground in their portrayal of gay and lesbian relationships

In recent years, drag queens and the Ballroom Scene have also been celebrated and brought back into public awareness through the hit TV show *RuPaul's Drag Race*. While the show has been groundbreaking in having drag recognized as a form of performance art by mainstream audiences, the real power of *Drag Race* has been in providing a display of queer culture for a *queer audience*. Through the show, talented and diverse performers such as Peppermint, Sasha Velour, Latrice Royale, and Shangela have become icons of queer culture, playing with and challenging society's ideas about gender. In their bold and charismatic expressions of individuality, the legacy of Marsha P. Johnson and the legendary children of the Ballroom live on.

Pushing The World Forward

In 1990, Justin Fashanu became the first British footballer to come out as gay. Fashanu was a promising young athlete, and had become one of the most successful black footballers of the 80s. Throughout his career, rumors about his sexuality had circulated among football clubs and fans.

Homophobia was rife in Britain at the time, and many people questioned whether a gay man should be welcome on the football pitch.

A dramatic backlash occurred when Fashanu came out publicly, and he became the target of relentless and horrific homophobic abuse. Tragically, Fashanu killed himself in 1998. It wasn't until 2014 that another footballer, Liam Davis, would publicly come out as gay.

Cultural ideas about what men and women are supposed to be and do are often very keenly felt by athletes, because ideas like leadership and athleticism are often very strongly connected to masculinity or maleness. People in sport who don't fit a narrow idea of what men or women should be like can find themselves bullied and excluded by teammates, or the target of homophobic abuse from fans. Coming out in such circumstances can be very hard indeed.

In 2009, Wales' Gareth Thomas became the first professional rugby player to announce he was gay

In 2009, Wales' Gareth Thomas became the first professional rugby player to announce he was gay. Thomas had an extremely successful rugby career both before and after coming out, and enjoyed a great deal of support from fans, teammates, and the sporting bodies to which he belonged. Shortly after he came out, during a game, fans of an opposing team struck up a homophobic chant about him, as a result of which the team received a hefty fine. Simply by making his identity public, Thomas brought about changes in the way rugby fans and players behaved—just like the Mattachines had done with bars and public attitudes in the 1960s. Thomas retired from rugby in 2011, but is a leading campaigner against homophobia in UK sports.

The first openly trans person to compete in professional sport was Renée Richards, who in 1977 scored an important victory after successfully suing the United States Tennis Association to be allowed to compete as a woman. Despite considerable controversy, Richards went on to enjoy a successful career as a tennis player and, later, a coach. Richards' court victory established an important precedent that allowed other trans athletes to push for acceptance in their particular sports, although they can still face serious opposition.

Mixed martial artist and trans woman Fallon Fox has faced almost constant controversy and discrimination since coming out in 2013, over whether or not she should be allowed to compete in women's divisions of her sport. While she received support from various sporting bodies, lawyers, and medical professionals, many voices within the MMA world wanted to see her barred from competition. Fox refused to back down, and, although she has not competed since 2014, her struggle against discrimination brought trans rights and trans identities out into public discussion. As she wrote in 2014: "I'm a transgender woman. I deserve equal treatment and respect to other types of women."

Sport is by no means the only arena in which being visibly queer can be difficult. The world of politics has long been another hotbed of homophobia and intolerance. Until very recently, the general public in most countries viewed being LGBTQ+ as a scandal, and politicians who came out would often lose their position or their jobs. The world has taken a long time to accept the idea of a queer person having any sort of power, so the achievements of queer politicians are particularly important for the community's liberation. In 1995, Georgina Beyer became mayor of Carterton, a town near Wellington, New Zealand, making her the first trans person to become a mayor. Later, in 1999, she became the first trans member of parliament. In 2009, Jóhanna Sigurðardóttir was elected prime minister of Iceland, becoming the first openly queer head of government in the world. Sigurðardóttir and her partner Jónina Leósdóttir were also among the first Icelandic couples to change their civil partnership to a marriage when marriage equality was achieved in Iceland in 2010.

All around us, in science, politics, sports, the arts, and every other industry, queer people are facing down prejudice and homophobia and steadily pushing the world forward.

> The world of politics has long been another hotbed of homophobia and intolerance

Having children or getting married are two things that can be fundamental to many people's idea of family. Other important things might include feeling loved, being supported, having people around you who care about you and who know you well, and having a home. Those are things that straight people may not have to think about very often—family is something that a lot of straight people can take for granted.

It's not been so easy for queer people though. Losing their family is just one of a number of very real risks that they have to deal with. Fear of the way parents or siblings might react is something that can make life for queer people not just hard, but occasionally unbearable.

For centuries, public opinion combined with medical attitudes and laws meant that someone could lose not just their family but their friends, their job, their freedom, or even their life if they were even suspected of being queer. Thanks to the work of queer activists, things slowly started to improve: laws changed, attitudes shifted, prejudices were abandoned. Gradually, in some parts of the world, queer people were granted rights that heterosexual people had never had to fight for.

But even that progress hasn't been universal. Still today, all over the world, LGBTQ+ people have to hide their identities because of what might happen to them if they come out. At the time of writing, homosexuality is illegal in around 70 countries, and carries the death penalty in eight. Laws and public attitudes in Russia and Saudi Arabia mean that being visibly queer is extremely dangerous. Even in places such as the USA, Canada, Australia, the UK,

and parts of Europe, where queer people are recognized and protected by law, homophobia and prejudice can still make life very difficult for LGBTQ+ people. Violent crime against members of the queer community, particularly trans people, remains a serious problem around the globe.

The journey toward equality has been a long and difficult one. There have been victories and tragedies, but along the way we've seen again and again how the power of the queer community to bring about change depends on queer people joining together, acting together, and shouting together, with one voice.

That journey isn't over. The struggle continues as we push for trans rights, for increased visibility for the bi and asexual communities, among others, as we push for and defend LGBTQ+ rights at home and overseas. Queer people have been leading the way but it's everyone's responsibility to offer support, and to call for change, recognition, and acceptance for LGBTQ+ people around the world. No one should have to live in fear because of who they are.

The rainbow flag is a symbol of hope and freedom, as well as a reminder and celebration of those who fought their own battles and blazed their own trails so that we could get where we are today. The queer community has its own history, its own traditions, its own space in society because it has fought hard for each one of those things, forcing the mainstream world to acknowledge them, forcing change.

Every queer life is part of that rainbow revolution, and every time someone comes out, they become a revolutionary.

	1867	**KARL ULRICHS'** SPEECH TO THE CONGRESS OF GERMAN JURISTS, MUNICH, GERMANY
OSCAR WILDE IS CONVICTED FOR GROSS INDENCY, UK	**1895**	
	1900	DEATH OF **OSCAR WILDE**
MAGNUS HIRSCHFELD OPENS THE **INSTITUTE OF SEXUAL SCIENCE**, BERLIN, GERMANY	**1919**	
HENRY GERBER FOUNDS THE SOCIETY FOR HUMAN RIGHTS, CHICAGO, USA	**1924**	**PERU** DECRIMINALIZES HOMOSEXUALITY
DEATH OF **LILI ELBE**, PIONEER OF TRANS RIGHTS	**1931**	
THE **INSTITUTE OF SEXUAL SCIENCE** IS SHUT DOWN BY THE NAZIS	**1933**	**DENMARK** DECRIMINALIZES HOMOSEXUALITY
ICELAND DECRIMINALIZES HOMOSEXUALITY	**1940**	
	1942	**SWITZERLAND** DECRIMINALIZES HOMOSEXUALITY
SWEDEN DECRIMINALIZES HOMOSEXUALITY	**1944**	
	1952	**ALAN TURING** ARRESTED AND CONVICTED FOR GROSS INDECENCY, UK
DEATH OF **ALAN TURING**	**1954**	
	1955	DEL MARTIN AND PHYLLIS LYON FOUND **THE DAUGHTERS OF BILITIS** IN SAN FRANCISCO, USA
THE MATTACHINE SOCIETY'S **"SIP-IN" PROTEST**, NEW YORK, USA	**1966**	THE **COMPTON'S CAFETERIA RIOTS**, SAN FRANCISCO
THE STONEWALL RIOTS, NEW YORK	**1969**	
THE FIRST **PRIDE MARCH**, NEW YORK THE UK'S **GAY LIBERATION FRONT** IS FOUNDED	**1970**	**AUDRE LORDE** PUBLISHES *CABLES TO RAGE*
DR H. ANONYMOUS'S SPEECH TO THE APA, TEXAS, USA	**1972**	
	1973	THE **APA** REMOVES "HOMOSEXUALITY" FROM THE DIAGNOSTIC AND STATISTICAL MANUAL OF MENTAL DISORDERS
HARVEY MILK IS ELECTED TO THE SAN FRANCISCO BOARD OF SUPERVISORS	**1977**	
HARVEY MILK IS ASSASSINATED, SAN FRANCISCO	**1978**	**THE RAINBOW FLAG** IS UNVEILED AT THE GAY FREEDOM DAY PARADE, SAN FRANCISCO
AUSTRALIA'S FIRST **MARDI GRAS**, SYDNEY	**1980**	

	1986	**LOU SULLIVAN** FOUNDS FTM, SAN FRANCISCO
LARRY KRAMER FOUNDS ACT UP, NEW YORK	**1987**	
	1988	**SECTION 28** VOTED IN TO BRITISH LAW
THE LGBTQ+ CAMPAIGN GROUP **STONEWALL** IS FOUNDED, UK	**1989**	
THE FIRST **AFRICAN PRIDE**, JOHANNESBURG, SOUTH AFRICA	**1990**	**ACT UP** PROTEST AT THE NATIONAL INSTITUTES OF HEALTH, BETHESDA, MARYLAND, USA
	1991	THE **RED RIBBON PROJECT** IS LAUNCHED AS PART OF THE CAMPAIGN AGAINST HIV/AIDS
THE **WORLD HEALTH ORGANIZATION** DECLASSIFIES HOMOSEXUALITY AS A MENTAL ILLNESS	**1992**	
	1994	**PIERRE SEEL'S** BOOK *I, PIERRE SEEL, DEPORTED HOMOSEXUAL* IS PUBLISHED, FRANCE
MURDER OF **RITA HESTER**, ALLSTON, MASSACHUSETTS, USA	**1998**	
	1999	**TRANS DAY OF REMEMBRANCE** IS FOUNDED, USA; **MONICA HELMS** DESIGNS THE TRANS PRIDE FLAG
THE **NETHERLANDS** BECOMES THE FIRST COUNTRY TO GRANT FULL MARRIAGE EQUALITY	**2000**	
	2003	**SECTION 28** REMOVED FROM UK LAW
THE FIRST **SAN FRANCISCO TRANS MARCH**	**2004**	
	2005	**SPAIN** LEGALIZES SAME-SEX MARRIAGE; **CANADA** LEGALIZES SAME-SEX MARRIAGE
SOUTH AFRICA LEGALIZES SAME-SEX MARRIAGE	**2006**	
WELSH RUGBY PLAYER **GARETH THOMAS** COMES OUT AS GAY	**2009**	**ICELAND** ELECTS THE FIRST OPENLY GAY HEAD OF GOVERNMENT IN THE WORLD
US PRESIDENT **BARACK OBAMA** ACKNOWLEDGES THE LGBTQ+ COMMUNITY IN HIS **STATE OF THE UNION** SPEECH	**2013**	**NEW ZEALAND** LEGALIZES SAME-SEX MARRIAGE; THE UK FULLY DECRIMINALIZES HOMOSEXUALITY
	2014	THE **UK** LEGALIZES SAME-SEX MARRIAGE
THE **US SUPREME COURT** DECLARES THAT SAME SEX MARRIAGE SHOULD BE LEGAL NATIONWIDE	**2015**	**IRELAND** LEGALIZES SAME-SEX MARRIAGE
	2017	**AUSTRALIA** LEGALIZES SAME-SEX MARRIAGE
INDIA DECRIMINALIZES HOMOSEXUALITY	**2018**	

Glossary

ACE, OR ASEXUAL: People on the asexual spectrum experience limited or no sexual attraction. Part of the LGBTQ+ community.

ACTIVISM: Taking a stand against an injustice; standing up and speaking out; being brave.

BI, OR BISEXUAL: Being attracted to people of more than one gender. Part of the LGBTQ+ community.

BINARY: A system where there are only two options; for example, boy–girl, male–female, gay– straight. Binary ideas often exclude identities that don't fit inside them (*see* Norms).

BUTCH: Looking and behaving in a strongly masculine way. Any gender can be butch (*see also* Femme).

COMING OUT: Telling someone that you are queer; correcting them when they have assumed that you are straight or cis, but you are not. Becoming revolutionary.

DRAG: Turning a certain gender identity into a larger-than-life, theatrical performance. Drag queens perform feminine genders while drag kings perform masculine genders.

EQUALITY: A situation where all groups of people have access to the same rights, the same services and the same protections as each other. A situation where everyone is safe and free from persecution. An ideal, a goal to strive for.

FAMILY: A group of people who love and support you.

FEMME: Looking and/or behaving in a strongly feminine way. Any gender can be femme (*see also* Butch).

FIERCE/FIERCENESS: Being fabulous, looking stunning in a way that is entirely true to yourself. Confidence, strength.

GAY: Being attracted to someone the same gender as you. Part of the LGBTQ+ community.

GENDER: Part of someone's identity, the way they think about themselves, not necessarily restricted to "boy" or "girl"/"man" or "woman" (*see* Trans). Also a social idea about what things like "men," "women," "boys," and "girls" are supposed to be, look like, or do. Sometimes people's own gender identity can be different from the one given to them by society. This can lead to conflict when they try to behave or look the way they want to (*see* Gender norms).

GENDER NORMS: What society expects from "men," "women," "boys," or "girls" in terms of what jobs they can do, where they can go or how they are supposed to look, act, or speak. Often used to advantage one gender over others (*see* Norms, Sexism).

GENDERQUEER: A gender identity that does not conform to normative views of gender. Genderqueer people may identify with both binary genders at the same time, or neither of them, or as something else entirely (*see* Trans). Part of the LGBTQ+ community.

HETEROSEXUAL: A man who is attracted to women, or a woman who is attracted to men. Societies in many parts of the world assume that this is the "natural" condition for people to be in, and oppress and persecute queer people as a consequence (*see* Norms).

HOMOPHOBIA: Any idea, action, or attitude that gives advantage to straight people over queer people. Often leads to queer people feeling unsafe.

INTERSEX: Someone whose biological sex does not easily fit in to the categories of "male" or "female." Part of the LGBTQ+ community.

LESBIAN: A woman who is attracted to women. Part of the LGBTQ+ community.

LGBTQ+: This stands for Lesbian, Gay, Bi, Trans, Queer/Questioning; letters representing the entire queer community. The plus sign at the end indicates that there are many other groups involved—you may see other letters included, such as I for Intersex, P for poly or pan, U for undecided, A for ace. You may see other ways of arranging the letters: BLGTQ, for example, or QUILTBAG.

MAINSTREAM: The majority-led, heterosexual world, where there are only two genders, "men" and "women," and they are expected to fall in love with each other, marry, and have children. Queer people do not fit easily into the mainstream.

MARRIAGE: A legal recognition of a relationship, traditionally restricted to heterosexual couples, but increasingly made available to same-gender partners. Freedom of choice to marry who you want to is considered a basic human right.

NON-BINARY (NB, OR ENBY): Having a gender identity that is something other than the standard, normative options of "man" or "woman." Part of the LBGTQ+ community.

NORMAL: What is most common in society, what most people experience, what most people do.

NORMS: Strongly held beliefs about what people should be like, or what they should do. Often the result of complex history and politics. People who don't follow society's norms are often oppressed (*see* Oppression).

OPPRESSION: Being treated unfairly, unkindly, badly by society. Not being free to be who you are. Living in fear.

PAN: Can refer to pansexual people, who are attracted to others regardless of their gender identity or biological sex, or to pangender people who express multiple gender identities at the same time. Part of the LGBTQ+ community.

POLY, OR POLYAMOROUS: People who want or have multiple romantic relationships at the same time. In poly relationships, everybody knows about everyone else's other partners. Poly people can be straight, bi, ace, or any other sexual identity.

PRIDE: A celebration of queer identity, history, and culture. An annual marker of the events centered around the Stonewall Inn in 1969. The first Pride was a riot.

QUEER: Not following society's norms around sex, gender, sexuality, or romantic relationships: not being straight. Queer is also a political idea, associated with radical activism in the LGBTQ+ community.

RAINBOW: A symbol of Pride and unity; a memorial for those who went before; a promise to the future.

SEXISM: Any idea, action, or attitude that gives advantage to one sex over the other, usually men over women.

STRAIGHT: *See* Heterosexual.

TRANS: Having a gender identity which is not what people expected of you at birth. Includes trans men, trans women, and also non-binary and genderqueer people (among others) (*see* Non-binary, Genderqueer). Part of the LGBTQ+ community.

TRANSITIONING: Changes made by a trans person in order to live as the gender with which they identify.

TRANSPHOBIA: Any idea, action, or attitude that discriminates against trans people. Often associated with violence and aggression (*see* Trans).

Index